The Last Kooradgie

Aborigines dancing. Drawing by Major Mitchell

THE LAST KOORADGIE

Moyengully, chief man of the Gundungurra People

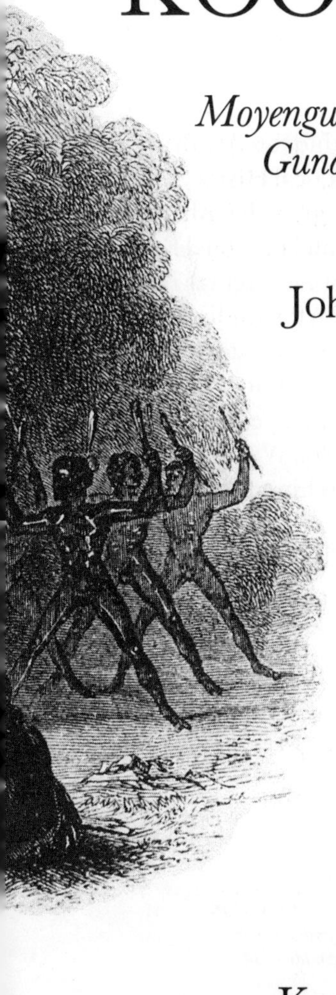

John Meredith

Kangaroo Press

For Brian Loughlin
who introduced me to Aboriginal culture

Acknowledgments

For assisting in my research I am greatly indebted to Bruce Knox, Ron Mills, John Low, Blue Mountains Local History Librarian, and Ian Tait, each of whom went to great lengths to obtain information and material on my behalf; and to Lionel Fowler and Jim Kohen for copies of the 'Return of Aboriginal Natives'. I would like to thank Mr Woolums of Picton for kindly allowing me to search his farmland while endeavouring to locate Moyengully's grave site, and Martin Fallding and Ian Tait for helping in that search. I am grateful to Frances Bodkin, Kaye Price and Robin Williams for their kindly advice, and to Zoe Wakelin-King of the Australian Museum for her help in searching for Moyengully's carved grave trees.

Two passages from Bernard O'Reilly's *Green Mountains* are quoted by kind permission of his daughter, Mrs Rhelma Kenny of Green Mountains, Queensland.

© John Meredith 1989

First published in 1989 by Kangaroo Press Pty Ltd
3 Whitehall Road (P.O. Box 75) Kenthurst NSW 2156
Typeset by G.T. Setters Pty Limited
Printed in Hong Kong through Bookbuilders Ltd

ISBN 0 86417 235 4

Contents

Introduction 7
Moyengully and Major Mitchell 16
   Tale of the Lost Pipe 20
Werriberri's Recollections 23
   Bernard O'Reilly on Billy Russell and the Lynches 27
The Cuneo-Carlon Stories 30
   When Moyengully was King 31
   An Ambassador Arrives 32
   Death and Interment of the King 33
   Civil War Threatens 34
   The Princess Gets Bewitched 36
   Rolfe Boldrewood Hollow 38
   Intrusion Upon a Bora 40
The End of a Culture 43
   Carved Trees at Picton 44
The Gundungurra Language 48
Gundungurra Mythology: Mirragan and Gurangatch 54
Anthology 60
   An Ode on King Murrungurry's Grave 60
   The Blackfellow's Grave 61
   Princess Betsy 62
   A Bushman's Experience 62
Bibliography 67
Appendix 68
Index 70

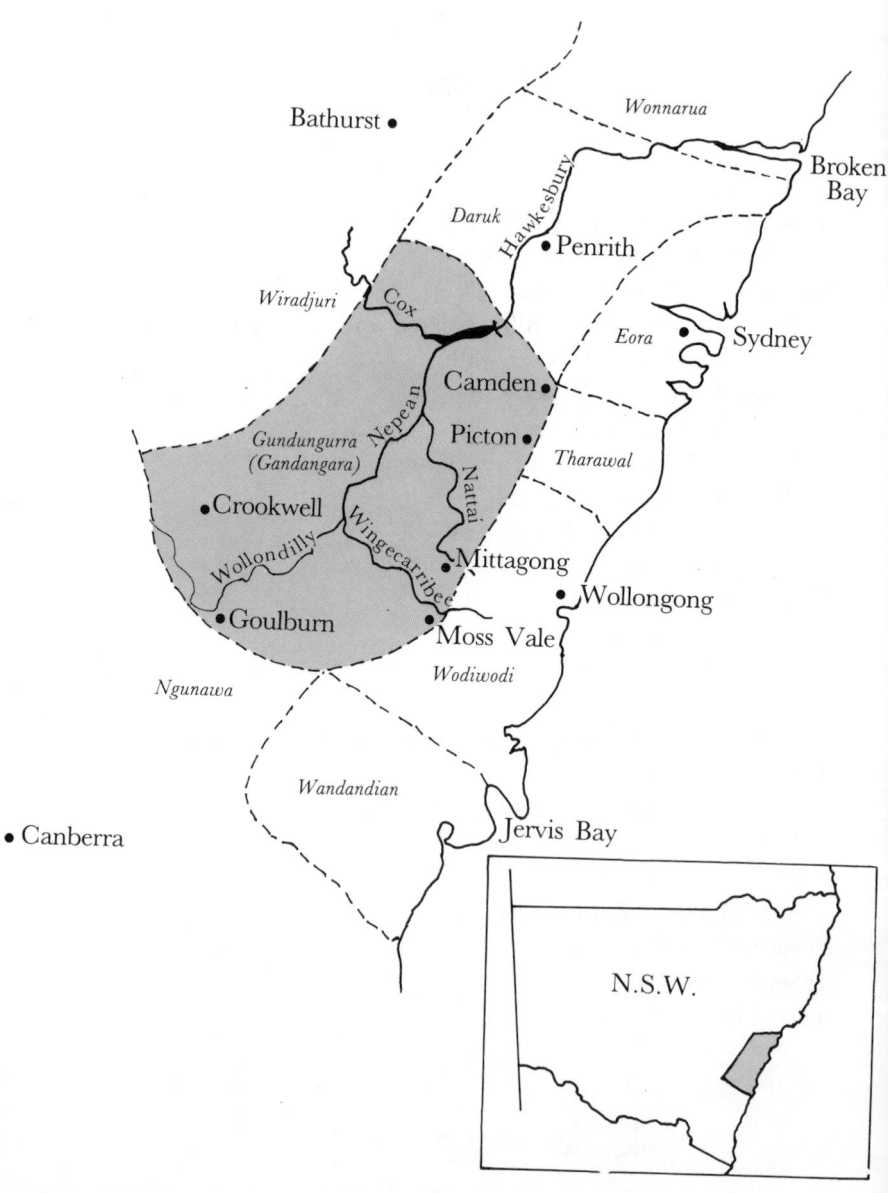

Gundungurra lands

Introduction

This book contains some words and phrases which may be offensive to Aboriginal people. They are not of my writing, but occur in accounts written by various 19th century authors. They should be taken as a reflection of social attitudes and English usage prevailing at that time. These items have been included because they constitute the only records of the Gundungurra people written down during the period when their traditional lands were being stolen from them.

Most of the stories are about Moyengully, a tribal elder and kooradgie of note, and they have been gathered from a number of sources. The book is not intended to be an anthropological survey, nor is it an historical study. It is a collection of reminiscences which make up a brief outline of the lifestyle of a group of people now gone forever.

The tribe of Aboriginal Australians called the Gundungurra, sometimes referred to as the Mountain People, or described as the Nattai Tribe or the Burragorang Tribe, occupied a tract of country lying at the north end of the Southern Highlands of New South Wales, and extending through the Blue Mountains to the slopes of the western side. The Gundungurra land was bounded in the east by the edge of the escarpment of the Great Dividing Range. From the vicinity of The Cowpastures near Camden in the north and extending over the Wingecarribbee Swamp and River near Moss Vale and Robertson, down to Goulburn in the south-west, it took in some remarkable natural features, such as the Wombeyan and the Jenolan Caves.

Only the kooradgies and other tribal elders would have known for certain where their country began and ended, but it certainly included areas like the lush, fertile valleys of Burragorang,

Megalong and Kanimbla, all teeming with bird and animal life, and favoured camping places for the tribe at certain seasons. Their neighbours to the north were the Dharrook tribe and on the south and south-east they were joined by the Thurrawal people.

Governor Macquarie noted two encounters with Aborigines in the Goulburn district in October 1820, when some of them joined his party of exploration. This was at the junction of the Gundary Creek with the Mulwaree Ponds. They presented him with five eels caught in the Mulwaree, and he noted their hardiness when they slept by their camp fires in the open, through a violent rain storm and with the thermometer standing at 39 degrees F. Hamilton Hume, in the following year, refers to the local Aborigines foraging for food between South Hill and North Hill in the same district, where there also existed a quarry for the manufacture of stone axes and other implements.

Of course the land did not belong to these people as the white man understands property ownership. It was the other way around. The people belonged to the land. Throughout their country were sacred sites—rocks, caves, rock-shelters or gibbergunyahs, ancient trees, streams and waterholes—and each was inseparably bound in with legendary spirit people of the dreamtime; each had its own special significance, its songs and ceremonies and its association with day-to-day living.

Like other Aboriginal people, the Gundungurra lived in complete harmony with the land and had a strong empathy with their environment, taking from it only what was necessary for food, shelter and warmth. After countless generations of occupation the land was virtually still in the same condition as their distant ancestors had found it on their arrival.

The tribe and its family groups had a communal life-style and were governed by the Law—the ancient tribal and family traditions. The Law was administered and enforced by a council of elders, consisting of the kooradgies or medicine-men, and the old men of the tribe. These elders were the tradition bearers, the custodians of a complex oral tradition of songs, dances, ceremonies and stories embodying the Law, which was sustained and passed on by them to the younger men. The old women of the tribe had ceremonies of their own to maintain the traditions of women's business, with their own particular songs, stories and dances.

Learning these traditions formed part of the education of every child, and young men and women were only initiated into adulthood when, on attaining puberty, they had been taught every aspect of the ancient rules that governed their lives.

Like other Australian Aborigines, the Gundungurra people were divided into sub-groups or moieties, referred to by themselves as 'skins', and a man could only marry certain women of a different skin from his own. The sub-groups were often divided into families or clans who camped together and moved through the tribal land hunting and gathering food as a unit.

Charles McAlister records that in his youth the Aborigines on the Tablelands, adjoining the Southern Highlands, were fairly numerous. He mentions three local tribes, the Mulwarrie, Tarlo and Burra Burra tribes. Of these the Burra Burras were the most warlike, their country including the Abercrombie district, Taralga and Carrabungla. He speaks of their fights with the Lachlan tribes. He refers to the Wollondilly (Gundungurra) tribe having its burying place on the hill above Lansdowne House.

The numerical strength of the tribe can only be conjectured—most likely it would have been several hundred, and the family units appear from description to have consisted of from ten up to perhaps fifty or sixty individuals.

McAlister states that the bora ceremony was performed upon a small red hill near the site of the present Kenmore Hospital, and goes on to say that at the first Goulburn horse races, in 1839, Aborigines outnumbered the white spectators by ten to one.

He then describes how, to celebrate the election of William Bradley as a member of the Legislative Council, a lunch was given at the Salutation Inn and, for the general public, Brodie had a bullock roasted in the market place. Duncan McKellar gave the bread and Bradley himself two hogsheads of ale. A large number of Aborigines was present at this event which took place on 14 June 1843.

The Gundungurra country was well watered by permanent streams, swamps, several large lakes and numerous waterholes, so there was always an abundant supply of food for the taking. Kangaroos, wallabies, walleroos, possums, bandicoots, wombats and a host of smaller animals provided red meat in plenty; there were emus, pelicans, ducks and pigeons; the streams abounded with eels, fish and yabbies, and the bush with snakes and lizards.

Fruit and vegetables were legion: *tdgerail* the lilly-pilly, *coo-yie* the native cherry, wild figs, bush currants, five corners, and dumplings or apple-berries. The women were adept in the use of the digging stick and could quickly turn up a dillybag of yams, ground-orchid bulbs or nutgrass corms; or, from the rotting logs in the gullies, a supply of fat, white bardie grubs; from the swamps came waterlily roots and stems. After treatment by leaching in water, the burrawang nuts, seeds of the macrozamia palm could be ground, made into cakes and roasted, and the fleshy pods of doobah were tasty either raw or cooked. Flower heads of banksia, bottlebrush, honeybush and waratah rinsed in a coolamon of cold water yielded a sweet, refreshing drink, and the nests of the small stingless native bee provided occasional hand-sized slabs of honeycomb.

James Backhouse describes meeting with Aborigines near a place where mountain limestone crops out, by the side of a chain of ponds, perhaps near Rocky Hill, and how one of the women was eating raw sow-thistles, as salad, with avidity.

The men hunted with a spear, thrown by the aid of a woomera or hooked spear-thrower, and with a *boolang* or throwing stick. In the warmer months clothes were an unnecessary encumbrance. During winter the chilliness of the highlands was mitigated by the use of cloaks or rugs made from wallaby or possum skins sewn together. Men sometimes used the spear-thrower as a pin to hold their cloak in position. The men often wore a headband of possum skin, fur side outward, and occasionally decorated their hair with the feathers of parrots. Major Mitchell described one young man who had a head dress of eagle feathers plaited into his hair.

Bennett describes several tribes or sub-groups camped on the

Goulburn Plains: some were in 'native costume' (meaning, one presumes, that they were naked) with an occasional extra dab of red ochre and the bolombine around the head. Others wore the yellow crest of the white cockatoo, pending from their beards. The women were glowing in grease and red ochre, their ringlets decorated with possum tails and the incisor teeth of the kangaroo. Some had the *cambun*, the bolombine of the Tumut country. Both men and women had raised cicatrices over the breast, arms and back. They were much amused at a bugle which they called a *cobbung* (large whistle).

When the Gundungurra first came to their land is not known. Certainly there were people in the area many thousands of years ago, as evidenced by the many examples of ancient red hand stencils in the rock shelters, but they may have been of a different race. Werriberri stated in 1914 that even the oldest men of the Gundungurra were unable to tell him the meaning of the red hands, nor could they say who had put them there. He was then 84 years of age, and was the last surviving tribal elder.

It is probably safe to assume that the Gundungurra or their forebears lived in the district for many thousands of years—some archeologists have put the figure at 40 000. If this is so, then their culture was already old when the Egyptians were first settling along the banks of the Nile, and the Incas were building their wonderful roads and temples in South America. Their religion was ancient long before the old Hebrews began to evolve a concept of their particular god, and before the coming of the prophets and seers whose teachings have coloured modern thought—Buddha, Christ, Confucius and Mahommed.

Forty thousand years—four hundred centuries—and still the land remained in the same state as when these people first came. A happy, healthy people, virtually free from disease, and possessed of all they needed for a life of fullness and plenty.

Then came the white man, the Anglo-Saxon with his 'superior civilisation'. One brief century of this civilisation sufficed to destroy a people and a culture. In Tasmania the usurpers came with guns and dogs. The taking over of the traditional lands of the Gundungurra people was less violent and more insidious, although there is a local oral tradition of John MacArthur herding a group of Aborigines into a gorge and shooting them. Although less brutal, the white settlers who moved into the Southern Highlands and the great valleys of the Blue Mountains were just as thorough in their genocide.

Having lived in isolation for such a vast period of time, the Aborigines possessed little or no resistance to European diseases. In the early years of colonisation, first an epidemic of smallpox, then influenza, diphtheria, measles, scarlet fever and tuberculosis wiped out an estimated thirty per cent of their people. Slower, but just as virulent, syphilis and gonorrhoea were responsible for thousands more deaths.

Dr George Bennett, in 1834, noticed that several of the Aborigines at Goulburn Plains had pits on their faces resembling those produced by smallpox, and which they informed him were caused by the disease in question. The name by which this disease is known among the Aborigines is *thunna thunna* or *tunna tunna*. He goes on to describe the symptoms, stating that the adults suffered more severely than the children, but that there were no deaths among the children.

The influenza epidemic of 1846 and 1847 accelerated the disappearance of the Aborigines, as they proved peculiarly susceptible to the disease. After the epidemic the Bench of Magistrates estimated the number of Aborigines in Goulburn in 1848 as 25. This was in a district where, a few years previously, the Aborigines had outnumbered the white settlers.

And they died for less obvious reasons. As the white settlers moved into the traditional tribal lands, clearing, cultivation, and the noise of their axes and guns drove away the birds and animals. Often the Aborigines were unable to follow the game into the more unsettled areas because these lay beyond their tribal boundaries. These boundaries were rigidly observed and already in 1802 the explorer Barrallier recorded that local Aborigines refused to guide him through the mountains because it would have involved trespass on the lands of neighbouring tribes.

With food sources depleted, the Aborigines were forced to depend more and more on handouts of rations of white man's tucker. The usual ration consisted of what the white man regarded as basic items of food: flour, sugar and tea. To this, some benefactors, more generous than others, or perhaps in return for work from the men or sexual favours from the women, added a fig or two of strong, dark twist tobacco, and a bottle or two of the obnoxious spirits then available under the name of rum or brandy, but actually distilled from wheaten or maize mash.

The effect of this starchy, sugary diet, almost devoid of protein and vitamins, upon a people used to living on fresh natural foods, rich in just those elements which were now lacking, was calamitous. The lean, active, athletic physiques depicted by Major Mitchell and other early 19th century artists, were soon replaced by grossly obese bodies, inactive and clothed in dirty, cast-off rags of their mentors, such as depicted by photographers of the 1890s and early 20th century.

Dr Waugh took the measurements of Yarraginny, a chief man of the Wollondilly tribe in 1848 and he expressed the opinion that such a perfectly formed man would scarcely be found in the British army.

In her book *Early Days of the Upper Murray* Jean Carmody puts forward another possible reason for the rapid decline in the Aboriginal population—the white man's gift of blankets, in many cases an official issue from the Government of the day. While the possumskin rugs were virtually waterproof, the blankets were not, and having no way of protecting them from rain and heavy dews, the Aborigines frequently slept under wet blankets, causing them to catch a chill and die of pneumonia.

So, degenerate, stripped of their dignity, besotted with crude alcohol, robbed of their traditional lands and the culture so closely associated with them, their sacred spirit-sites such as Wombeyan and Jenolan caves desecrated and turned into tourist venues, their bodies sick and rotting with the white man's diseases, ennervated by his poisonous tucker, they had nothing left to live for. So they died.

Four hundred centuries of tradition wiped out by one century of 'civilisation'. And as I wrote these words, after a further hundred years of 'development', we were being called upon by our media and our politicians to celebrate our bicentennial. What were we supposed to celebrate? Would not a year of contrition have been more to the point?

One of the tribal elders of the Gundungurra during the early part of the 19th century was a man named Moyengully. Possessed of outstanding qualities and with a strong personality, most of the white people who came into contact with him were moved to record the event in writing. He is said to have resented the white man's intrusion into Gundungurra territory; he was a bold fighter and was held in great regard by his peers, but apparently he realised the futility of trying to repel the invasion with violence.

Some of these stories about Moyengully were related by Ben Carlon to William Cuneo of Thirlmere during the 1890s when they were partners in silver mining ventures at Yerranderie in the Burragorang Valley, where Carlon was born in 1841 into one of the pioneer families, and where he grew to manhood. It is ironic that the discovery of the silver-lead ore was made by an Aborigine, Werriberri, and his mate Billy George in 1871, and it was the ensuing rush for mining leases that completed the alienation of the Gundungurra country.

Going by Carlon's birthdate, Moyengully's induction or election as a kooradgie and leading tribal elder would have taken place in the mid to late 1840s. The occasion when young Ben Carlon accidentally stumbled upon the bora ceremony was soon after he left school, and thus about 1855. The fact of the fire burning in a tree, as described in this story, suggests that the Aborigines may have been engaged in the Evening Star ceremony, in a manner similar to the one held in the Northern Territory, which also involved a fire lit in the fork of a tree.

In his book *Recollections*, Werriberri, or Billy Russell, states that Moyengully was his uncle. Since Billy's father was a white man, the old kooradgie could only have been his mother's brother, and therefore Werriberri's symbolic father or tribal guardian, whose responsibility it would have been to educate the lad in tribal law, hunting skills and fighting, or as the tribesmen put it, to grow-him-up.

As Moyengully was born about 1800, he would have been about 30 when Werriberri was born in 1830—soon after Major Mitchell sketched Moyengully's portrait—and would have been in his mid-40s when he became a kooradgie.

The use of British imperial terminology by Cuneo, Carlon and other 19th century writers, e.g. 'King', 'Queen' and 'Princess', reflects English usage of the period, and an attitude exemplified by the quaint custom of issuing 'King-plates' to chief men of the tribes. These took the form of a brass medallion breast-plate, with a neck chain, generally in the shape of a crescent or a shield, engraved with the King's 'Christian' name, and sometimes the name of the benefactor and the date.

Somebody, probably William Redfern Antill of 'Abbotsford', who was known to the Gundungurra people as 'Mister Willy', gave Moyengully a breastplate. After his death this was kept at 'Jarvisfield', the other Antill residence, for about a hundred years, but was then sold at auction with other family effects.

John Meredith
13 April 1988

Moyengully and Major Mitchell

The Gundungurra's first experience of the white invaders was when emancipated convict John Wilson went to live with them in 1792. Wilson was a young man, a former mariner who, in October 1785, at Wigan in Lancashire, was convicted of having stolen nine yards of cotton cloth, valued at tenpence, and was sentenced to transportation for seven years. He reached Australia on board the Alexander, *a transport of the First Fleet, in January 1788.*

When Wilson's term expired at the end of 1792, he took to the bush and lived with the Gundungurra people in the Bargo–Picton Loopline district on and off for several years. He was known to the Aborigines as Bun-bo-e, developed an intermediate language between his own and theirs, and travelled about with them over much of the country within 150 km of Sydney Town.

Later he returned to Sydney, and subsequently led two journeys of exploration in the Picton–Mittagong area. These expeditions produced the first specimen of the lyrebird and the first report of the koala. Wilson's strange career ended in 1800. He had reverted again to his wild life and, according to reports, had risen to a position of importance in the tribe of his adoption. When he attempted to take a young woman of the tribe for his wife, a disagreement occurred and he was speared by one of the elders. Perhaps he had tried to marry a woman of the wrong 'skin', or one who had already been promised in marriage, either of which would have been unacceptable.

Moyengully was born about the same time as Wilson's death, and was named after the place where he was born in the vicinity of Connors Plains on the Bathurst side of the mountains. He died near Picton on 12 October 1858. The earliest recorded description of him came from Major Mitchell, *the government surveyor-general, during the winter of 1828, when he wrote in his field note book about the tribe camped near him at the foot of Mount Gibraltar in the vicinity of Mittagong:*

'1828. Saturday, May 31st... After dinner I learned that the King of Nattai had "sat down" near my encampment, and in the evening I went to his fires; there were several young men at different fires—one black woman with her husband and child at another—and a widow with two children at another. Moyengully, the King, sat at another fire. He had a swelling on his right wrist and asked me for something to cure it. Several native spears stood against a tree beside him, and as many more were laid on the ground, but he got up and set them also against the tree.

'The young men, who lay between *three* fires were of a gay disposition that night, for they sung several songs. One was what they called The Bathurst Song, another The Kangaroo Song—each line commencing "Kangaroo-oo". One commences and the others join in the words et c.—the old King added his bass voice occasionally to the strain. One young fellow seemed one of the happiest beings I ever saw—without any covering but a skin over his hips, he lay on his belly on the ground, laughing heartily occasionally and playing his legs carelessly about as he lay. His hair behind was filled with a profusion of black Eagle's feathers, which had a very appropriate or good effect...

'Sunday 1st June. The King of Nattai having come to the tents I could not resist the temptation of drawing his head, the profusion of woolly locks seemed so extraordinary. He sat to me very impatiently; I promised him a pair of trowsers, and one of the men brought him a pair of Parramatta cloth but he refused them, saying that they were not fit for a gentleman. A good new pair of grey cloth were then offered him but he refused them also—saying he wanted a pair like mine, pointing to them. I gave him a pair of thin ones which he accepted and thanked me for. I would have drawn the feathered dandy too, but he had gone that morning towards the Cow Pastures—"to look about" as they said.'

Mitchell then persuaded 'Billy' Yerramagang to sing over the Kangaroo Song several times while he wrote down the words, first in the Gundungurra language and then Yerramagang's translation into English.

Kangaroo Song

Gubi gubi gay gin ganba aei ganba geba gure gruen gay,
(Spear thrown but misses the kangaroo)
Arabun uma enimya aray inglay wanumbula ingay enimili ingay,
(Can't find kangaroo)
Midme gurga enga mamega gangeroo abona tinnua eria cobua na nalluderra luba,
(Kangaroo looks but sees nobody)
Burranbunga windeginye uringango kuto oringa tumberin gang cumbiaga.
(Kangaroo turns away and the hunter kills it.)

(Kangaroo is not an Aboriginal word but was mistakenly assumed to be their name for the animal by one of Captain Cook's seamen. Later the Aborigines came to accept the word as being the white man's name for it.)

On the same day as the Surveyor-General took down the Kangaroo Song, and drew the pencil portrait of Moyengully, he took down the words of another song. It was about the Great Road South, the construction of which Mitchell was overseeing on this occasion. Doubtless the song was intended to accompany a corroboree that lampooned the white-man roadworkers.

Road Song

Morudá yerrabá tundaj kmara,
Morudá yerrabá tundaj kmara,
(Road goes creaking long shoes)
Morudá yerrabá meniyonging white ma la,
Morudá yerrabá meniyonging white ma la.
(Road goes uncle and brother white man see.)

Moyengully, drawn by Major Mitchell

The noting down of these two songs probably constitutes the first instance of the field collection of traditional songs in Australia. Mitchell always showed a deep interest in the Aborigines and their way of life, and made friends with them whenever the opportunity presented itself. In his book Three Expeditions into the Interior of Eastern Australia *published in 1838, he makes one more reference to Moyengully and his Gundungurra people:*

'... In the numerous ravines surrounding Jellore, the little river Nattai has its source, and this wild region is the haunt and secure retreat of the Nattai tribe, whose chief, Moyengully was one of my earliest Aboriginal friends.'

The Tale of the Lost Pipe

The Gundungurra people were possessed of a strong sense of self esteem. Thus, Moyengully gently asserted his rank to Mitchell by declining to accept a pair of shoddy trousers as payment for posing, but, in keeping with his rank as a kooradgie, demanded a pair equal in quality to Mitchell's best. Similarly, an anonymous Aborigine placed more importance on recovering a lost smoking pipe than in getting the Surveyor General back to his camp in time for supper. The story is related in Assistant Surveyor W.R. Govett's manuscript note book for 1828–35:

When we were encamped at the head of the Wollondilly River in the County of Argyle a ludicrous circumstance happened to Major Mitchell which shews how much the Black values a broken tobacco pipe.

Major Mitchell one morning left the tents accompanied with one Blackfellow and two of our men to proceed to a mountain about 6 miles distant, but which was not accessible to horses owing to the broken nature of the interjacent country.

On their arrival the Surveyor General lost no time in taking advantage of the position of the hill in sketching and taking angles, being determined to prevent the necessity of his going there a second time. About an hour or so before sunset Mitchell, having finished his work descended to the spot where the men had made a fire and got a pot of tea ready &c. and as soon as they had taken their repast all started for the tents.

They travelled along having the Black as their guide, up one hill, down another, crossing ravines, thick scrubs and rocky places for some time very contentedly, although it had been dark for an hour. Mitchell's patience however at last became exhausted and he broke the silence by saying to one of the men—'I wonder if this black rascal is taking us the way we came; we ought to be near the tents by this time; by God I'll trust no man in future, but take the lead myself. Here, come back!' addressing the Black, 'Are you taking us to the tents? And have we to go up that damn black mountain?'

'Me make allight directly, me sit down tent directly—this way Major,' and saying this off the Black trotted and hastening the party up the mountain which Mitchell was not satisfied that he had passed before.

Up they went, puffing and blowing and making now and then an oath of discontent and damning the Black for walking so fast as they proceeded. At last Mitchell again became angry and feeling satisfied that the Black had been taking them a different route, stopped the party and again addressing the Black, asked him in an angry tone—'Where were the tents?' 'Me find him directly,' and then pointed as they thought probably to where the tents might be, for Mitchell had been so confounded as to the country he had been travelling and it being now so extremely dark, scarcely knew the actual direction of the Encampment.

'Damn you!' said he to the Black, 'are we to cross that infernal mountain too?'

'Bale (no) Major, me find him directly'—and after walking a hundred yards or so, they found themselves (to their astonishment and bitter annoyance) by the fire where, nearly three hours before, they had taken their tea when Mitchell had finished his work on the Mountain.

The burst of Mitchell's anger was prevented by the Black

jumping and capering, crying out—'Me got him! Me got him!'

'Got what?'

'Budgery pipe, oh murry budgery pipe!' and shewing at the same time a little black, filthy pipe about 3 inches long—for which, when the Black found he had left it behind, he brought Mitchell and his men all the way back by a different route. 'Now,' said the Black, 'Me make map and you go tent directly.'

Werriberri's Recollections

Werriberri was said to be the son of Major Russell of Regentville. He died on 4 April 1914, aged 84 and thus was born in 1830. He is buried in the Roman Catholic cemetery at Camden. In the Return of Aboriginal Natives, *taken at Picton in 1842, there is listed a boy, 'Probable age 7, name Werriberrie, English name Yellow John', and this is probably the same person. Perhaps he was five years younger than he thought, or then perhaps he may have been just small for his age.*

His Recollections *was published in 1914 as a pamphlet written down for him by A.L. Bennett of Glenmore. Werriberri is described as a chiefman of the 'Gun-dun-gorra' Aborigines of the Burragorang Valley, and his English name is given as Billy Russell. He is stated to have died soon after publication of the booklet, a few paragraphs from which now follow:*

My earliest recollections are naturally of my mother, Wonduck, named after the place where she was born, near Richlands, which was the general custom in the tribe of my race, that is, the Gun-dun-gorra, though Wonduck's husband being named Muroon* which is the name of the wild cucumber vine[1] bearing oblong berries called Moombir and which are of a brown colour when ripe. The vines are rather plentiful in stringybark country.

My uncle was My-an-garlie, wrongly called Mullun-gully by whites. My-an-garlie, my uncle became principal man of our tribe about 50 years ago. His chief camping ground being in the Burragorang Valley. My-an-garlie was the Aboriginal name of a locality near the place now known as Connor's Plains near Bathurst.

---

* *Spelled Murruin in records and by Cuneo.*
[1] *Billardiera scandens:* Dumplings or Common Apple Berry.

Werriberri, photographed by Roy Dowle

The chief man before him that I can remember being a very old blind man whose name I have forgotten, and then 'Old Boyne' who was a clever man either with the spear, boomerang or shield as well as feats of strength and fighting. I have also heard the name of Goondel mentioned as an early chief man.

I was born on the banks of the Werri-berri Creek, near where Mrs. Felix O'Hare's farmhouse now stands and I can remember my mother carrying me on her back cuddled down in a fold of her 'possum's skin rug folded across her shoulders. I felt quite safe and comfortable, as any young Burru (Kangaroo) in his mother's pouch. Many times when travelling and I was crying for a drink, she would, when near water, quench my thirst by filling her mouth at the stream and then give it to me from her mouth to mine.

Murro-lung-gulung is a place where a hand was stencilled on a rock cave. I never knew what was the meaning of the hand on the rocks, but old natives said they were very very old indeed and were in some way connected with the Bulan, an Aboriginal God. Red earth is bulber—oxide of iron—and it was roasted in the fire to give a brighter colour then mixed with fat or gease.

Cubbitch-barta is the name of the Cowpastures tribe, from barta, pipe clay, plenty. The old Aborigines about Camden were a different tribe to those of Burragorang. 'Old Bundle' was the chief man of that tribe, and Gur-gur being the name of their language, while that of ours was Gundun-gorra.

Murrandah was the name of the chief man of the sub tribe at Burru Burru, Richlands. I have seen it printed in a semi-government paper that he was killed in a fight with the Burragorang tribe of blacks in 1844.* I can remember Murrandah as I was about 15 years of age when he died. The fight really was between he and another man and was not a tribe fight at all. Sub-tribes never fought against each other but only against men of other tribes, such as the Wiraijuri tribe, north

---

* *This fight was mentioned in the Cuneo/Carlon story, in which they described Moyengully as having killed somebody in a tribal fight. It would have been when Ben Carlon was 5 or 6, about 1846. Werriberri was born about 1830, so would have been about 15 at the time.*

and west of Bathurst, those of the south of Yass and the coast tribe Dharruck and the Camden tribe, Cubbitch-Batha.

Werriberri's grave in Camden

Bernard O'Reilly on Billy Russell and the Lynches

Bernard O'Reilly's forebears were among the first settlers to take up Gundungurra land for farming in the early part of the 19th century. Most of the people who followed the O'Reillys and the Carlons into the vast, fertile valleys of Burragorang, Megalong and Kanimbla in the heart of the Blue Mountains were Irish, such as the Flanagans, the Ryans and the Kellys.

O'Reilly has set down his memoirs in two strongly evocative books, Cullenbenbong, *and later,* Green Mountains. *Although he was only a lad when Werriberri was an old man, he had an affection for the old Aborigine and wrote feelingly about the Gundungurras and their musical language.*

...Visitors to our house were always welcomed by old and young, but we kiddies specially liked anyone out of the common, such as the Hindus or perhaps one of the old blacks who came around. The blacks, as we remember them, used to wander around the local districts drifting from one small job to another. Their womenfolk were capable of washing or heavy housework, but seldom stayed long in one place; the men were hard workers spasmodically, but they lacked the gift of application. There was small inducement for them to be otherwise. White man took their lands and natural food, made them accept a new way of living, yet prepared no place for them in the new order. If black man became a drifting derelict it is to white man's shame.

The older men—some of whom had been great men in a tribal sense—were mostly too feeble for work of any duration, but they found many little ways of earning tucker and 'baccy'. They knew white man's little likes and preferences and they traded on them. Old Billy Russell, last king of the Burragorang blacks, who fairly often got over our way in his old age, never came empty handed. Sometimes he'd bring half a sugar bag of the highly-prized snow white pipe clay from over Megalong way—our pipe clays were a dirty cream colour and Billy knew that a woman loves snowy clay wash for her fireplace. That little gift was good for a week's tucker from Mother's precious store and a plug of black tobacco from Dad's shelf.

When he was older and not well enough to carry weight he would bring a lovely bunch of waratahs from Medlow Gap country as he came over Black Dog. Waratahs didn't grow within miles of Cullenbenbong, and how well that old man knew my family's weakest spot. Another time he came by the sandstone benches above Megalong and brought a huge bunch of the wiry Curly Cane that grows there. Curly Cane makes the best and most durable of all bush brooms, but none grew nearer than Megalong.

Old Billy and Fanny Lynch came more frequently, but of course they seemed part of the family. Fanny was Grandmother's help long before Mother was born, and Billy as a youth worked for Grandfather, but when they became too old for regular work they too drifted with the restlessness of their kind.

Dear old Fanny who loved Mother and had nursed her as a baby would come in shyly first and say, 'I come to see if I can do something for you, Mizzes; Billy come along too, he been gettin' some nesses'. Sure enough there'd be Billy partly hiding behind the shed and holding a huge cogie full of lovely white honey in the comb. There was no doubt that he'd been robbing some bees 'nesses'.

That was quite a feat for an old man; the nest might have been forty feet up in a hollow limb. First Billy would find a stringybark tree with a big bump or cogie on it. Billy would cut the bark in a circle all round the cogie and then skilfully strip it off. That would give him a fine bark dish. This done he'd climb to the nest and sit straddled on the limb while he chopped it out, then, unmindful of bees and stings, he'd scoop out the honey comb and drop it to Fanny; who'd catch it in the cogie.

...Billy would select bits of fine goose down and then take a wee bit of honey from the store. Thus mysteriously armed he'd go down to where the bees were watering in the gravel by Long Swamp. Dipping bits of the snowy down in honey he's stick pieces on the backs of various bees and climb up the bank to a vantage point and wait for them to fly. With that miraculous eyesight which is black man's chief asset he'd watch that spot of white until it disappeared over a distant ridge. Marking the spot on the ridge by a boulder or stump Billy would hastily dab more down on newly arrived bees, then run for the ridge and stand waiting by his landmark. The next marked bee would probably show the way to the very tree where the nest was, for in well-watered country bees do not go far to water. There would be muffled chopping in the distance and later Billy would turn up with another cogie of honey.

Perhaps they would stay a week, perhaps a month, or more, but sooner or later in spite of Mother's entreaties they would wander aimlessly off to westward and the sunset of their tribe.

An excerpt from Cullenbenbong *by Bernard O'Reilly.*

The Cuneo-Carlon Stories

William Albert Cuneo was born in 1860 at Binalong, where he spent his childhood. He was station master at Thirlmere from 1885, and also postmaster from 9 May 1887, until about 1907, and he died at Stanmore in 1942.

An amateur author and poet, he composed and published several ballads as broadsides, and also wrote a number of essays and a couple of plays. He contributed collected texts to Banjo Paterson's Old Bush Songs, *was interested in the history of the local Aborigines and became involved in silver mining ventures at Yerranderie in the Burragorang Valley in partnership with Bernard Patrick Carlon, who was born in 1841 at Carlon Town, also in Burragorang Valley.*

Carlon related to Cuneo many stories about his childhood adventures with the Gundungurra natives in Burragorang. Cuneo published some of these reminiscences, with acknowledgement to Carlon, in the Picton Post and Advocate *in 1893. Later he expanded them into several longer stories, but failed to acknowledge the source of his information; in fact he has written them in such a manner as to suggest that the incidents related happened during his own childhood in the Burragorang Valley, but we know that he was born and grew up in the Binalong district.*

The following stories, as set down by William Albert Cuneo, should then be regarded as the reminiscences of Ben Carlon. Throughout his writing, Cuneo refers to Moyengully as 'Murrungurry', and gives as his authority William Redfern Antill of Abbotsford, who used to issue rations to the last remnants of the tribe and who insisted that 'Murrungurry' was the correct way to pronounce the name. Since Werriberri corroborates Mitchell's usage of Moyengully, although with a slightly different accent, I have adhered to the earliest written record.

When Moyengully was King

I think I was about four years old when Dad (Patrick Carlon) bought the farm at Burragorang, then the headquarters of the Kamileroi tribe that claimed sovereignty over a tract of country much larger than the present County of Camden. We were ploughing, or rather Dad was. I only played in the furrows he made, when the tall, powerful-looking white-haired blackfellow wearing a kind of tiara about his head made in a curious fashion from possum's wool, came accompanied by about 20 others armed to the teeth and almost angrily enquired, 'What for you do this ferra?' 'This my land, I plough him now, by and by I sow him corn,' answered Dad, somewhat amused.

'My land. My corn. You sow him, I take him by and by,' said the old man hautily. Dad was taken aback but he answered softly, 'Very well. By and by you come along. Plenty feller corn makit budgery damper. I give it you. Plenty good feller you.' It appeared to appease the old man; he spoke to his followers, they grunted in approval, then walked away.

He kept his word. Before the corn was ripe, they camped close by and commenced to help themselves. Dad was too wise to do more than remonstrate against their extravagance and by gentle persuasion at last succeeded in getting on friendly terms with them.

I too became the playmate of little Princess Queahgang. We did not know that she was a princess then. Well do I remember her chubby little black face and piercing black eyes that looked at you through a mass of tousled black curls. Mother just loved to wash her face and hands and often bribed her with toffee made from honey and butter to let her comb out her tangled, jet-black tresses. We roasted corn cobs; sometimes mother boiled them, and we had feasts in the cubby house that Dad rigged for us with bushes thrown over the corner of the stockyard fence.

I often wonder why and regret why we did not enquire about her family history, but the fact is that these people were always very reticent and loathe to answer questions, and I often think they divined your thoughts and gave answers that they considered would satisfy you but which were far from the truth. I do not wish to infer that they were studied liars, indeed I found them truthful in almost every instance, but this was habitual with them when you questioned them about their religions or their tribal ceremonies.

For instance, Mother used to ask the gins about their marriage laws but they only grinned and said very little. We know that there was one we called King, a Kooradgie or Doctor, but we never heard of a Queen, although a King had two wives or gins as they were called. Dad would not allow us to go to the camp. He was afraid that we might be poking our noses into other people's business and innocently give offence.

An Ambassador Arrives from Edwards River

It was about this time that a great event took place. A blackfellow came with a message from the tribe of the Edwards River. He carried neither a spear, boomerang or nulla, but never went without a peculiar carved stick. He did not go to the King's camp immediately he arrived; he remained about a quarter of a mile off. Dad tried hard to buy the stick from him and offered him big-fellow money, but it was useless and when Dad would press his offer, the stranger would depart.

He was supplied with food and signals were sent to all tribal units by the King, to their respective hunting grounds by means of fire and smoke signals drawn through sheets of curled bark. When all the units were assembled, this great ambassador, for such he really was, delivered his message. Afterwards a great corroboree was held, then the ambassador was escorted to the boundary of the Kamilaroi dominions.

We were unable to find out what the message was about. I'm sure the gins did not know or mother would have wormed it out of them. Yet they appeared excited and very pleased for days past, but they were always like that when a corroboree was about to take place. They composed the songs for it and sang them to the music of drums made by folding possum rugs. Dad reckoned the corroboree was like our theatre is to us, therefore, nothing to wonder at.

Death and Interment of the King

A few months after this event took place the old king died and weird lamentations were heard for many days and especially after dark at the various camps situated on both sides of the river. The gins disfigured their faces with wattle gum and ashes. The king was tied in a sitting posture, evidently before the rigours of death took place and was placed in the grave in a sitting position with his face turned to the east.

The grave was dug with sharp pointed sticks and must have entailed a great deal of labour. It was round and about three feet in diameter. All his treasures were buried with him. Over the corpse, bark and sticks were placed and then the earth was filled in and stones also and two old men tramped upon it, thus ramming it as tightly as possible. Three trees were carved and the carvings too faced the east. A kooradgie had charge of this and directed the work of two men, but one act he did alone.

This represented peculiar curved lines. The others were of the usual herring-bone pattern. I have since been told of this peculiar kind of carving. It is only put on the trees where a King or a descendant of the royal line is buried, and that the kooradgie can tell in what degree the interred person was by the markings on the trees. That is to say that certain carved lines either in form or number represent these particulars. This was told to me by the last remaining kooradgie of the Burragorang blacks.

Around the camp where the King died small mounds of ashes were heaped up and soon after his interment small fires were lighted and the kooradgies with all the men of the tribe assembled.

Green leaves were thrown on the fires to create smoke. The kooradgies stood in front carrying their dilly bags or charm bags in their hands and proceeded to invoke the aid of all the departed spirits of bygone tribesmen in avenging the death of the King. Every death that took place was believed to be due to the agency of evil spirits sent by another tribe.

The ceremony was witnessed by all the men of the tribe, who stood in rows behind the kooradgies. The wind began to blow and at a signal from the kooradgies all eyes were turned in that direction, then the kooradgies began to gesticulate violently, and pandemonium reigned generally. Spears, boomerangs and nullas were pointed in the direction that the wind was blowing and vengeance vowed on the evil ones who came that way and stole the spirit of the king.

Civil War Threatens

A great civil war was threatened over the election of a successor to the deceased King. There were two claimants for the throne. One was called Murruin and the other was Murrungurry, or as Major Mitchell calls him, Moyengully, who was Queahgang's father. Both had certain claims but in what way I do not understand. The gins were very concerned and shook their heads sadly and told Mother they were afraid of big feller fight. The whole tribe were assembled and father and I were allowed to see the piealler.*

A long line or avenue was formed by the blackfellows who knelt on one knee on either side. Their bodies were painted with oxide of iron with occasional white stripes alternating. These were drawn longitudinally across the chest with pipe clay obtained from between layers of the Hawkesbury sandstone and coal measures that abound in that district. Their hair was stuffed with gay coloured parrots' feathers, those from the red King Parrot

* *Pieller: Apparently a Gundungurra word for a big meeting.*

predominating. It was a weird scene. They all leaned together with heads bent and supported by one hand resting on one knee. They all kept their gaze fixed on the ground.

Between the rows the chief men, two at a time, one of them a kooradgie, walked up and down and addressed the men. Judging by the gestures, by no means ungraceful, they made vigorous speeches. None spoke but those privileged by their rank, and acclamations were attended by grunts and the most successful speakers were they who got the most grunts simultaneously. It was a big feller piealler and no mistake. The deliberations lasted about two hours and then a very big blackfellow was led to the opposite end of the avenue by two of the most successful speakers. He wore a tiara made from possum's wool wound around his head in the same fashion as the late King.

Immediately he appeared, all the blackfellows kneeling down rose and by a quick and graceful movement crossed their spears, and the King walked down the avenue with a chief man or kooradgie on either side of him. I thought he looked very dignified as he walked slowly down beneath the arch of spears. This was Moyengully. He faced about when he reached the end of the aisle and stood very still and erect. The Pretender Murruin was then led in and all his arms were taken from him. I began to be afraid that they were going to kill him. The men resumed their kneeling position and Moyengully addressed him, very angrily, I thought. It was a short address and the grunts he received were very unanimous. Poor Murruin. He was banished.

A small tract of land was given to him to hunt on near Picton. From off it he never dared to roam. To do so and be caught meant certain death. Here he was known to the whites as King Peter. He soon fell a victim to the rum bottle. Also his gin, the only companion allowed in his exile.

The late W.R. Antill Esquire, of Abbotsford, Picton, told me that a few days before Peter died, he was speaking to him and Peter said, 'Me soon tumble down now, Mister Willy, I think'. 'Ah, nonsense! Why do you think like that Peter?' 'Me see old Mary along the mill last night.' Mary, his gin, died at the mill some time previously. 'Ah, too much rum, Peter. White fellow see too much also when belly full of rum.' However the Pretender was found dead at the old mill a few days afterwards.

Not many weeks after Moyengully was elected King, a neighbour of ours got an awful fright. About thirty blacks with gins and piccaninies arrived at the house about midnight, each one carrying a firestick, and took possession of the house immediately he opened the door to enquire what the matter was. They were all in great terror. The gins wailed piteously and the men crouched down silent and haunted looking. They absolutely refused to move a foot when requested to do so.

The gins said that a big feller fight had taken place near Camden but their men had been beaten, although Moyengully killim three fellers. It was then remembered the wind blew smoke from the funeral fires from the direction of Camden. Further enquiries elicited the fact that the fight was in revenge for the death of the King, that Moyengully had distinguished himself, and was held in great reverence and awe ever afterwards, particularly by women.

The Princess Gets Bewitched

A few years flew quickly and Princess Queahgang became a comely young gin. She often came to help Mother, indeed Mother tried to keep her always and offered to pay her. Sometimes she stayed quite contentedly for two months, and then would suddenly say that she wanted to go walkit about. Mother also observed that prior to this declaration she would take a fancy to some dress she wore and she would often find her looking at it. She invariably asked for this article and when she obtained it would almost immediately depart.

One day a young blackfellow came and told Mother that Queahgang was cobbawn, sick. Mother, who had a kind of motherly love for her, was very disturbed, and made many enquiries from the gins who affirmed that she was ill and that the chief kooradgie would have to be made good again, because he failed to suck a stone from her arm which was supposed to be the cause of her illness. Then came another report that Queahgang was bewitched by a spirit, that came in the form of a bird called Twan and had to be carried about.

This was too much for mother. She started for the camp, taking a bottle of castor oil and some painkiller with her and other simple remedies that she knew of. These things cured her and I was sent to the camp with soup and cornflour pudding and other little dainties every day until she grew quite convalescent. Although very undemonstrative, I am quite certain they appreciated our kindness and to what extent the following pages will reveal.

One incident I mention because we did not notice it at the time and because it is very unusual, and will serve to illuminate that which transpired long afterwards. A young blackfellow used to come to cut a bit of wood for Mother, and if the buckets were empty, would take such as were empty and go to the river and fill them. He also appeared to like to do it without attracting any notice. Mother appreciated it too, because Dad was away from home at the time, and when Dad came home she told him about it and made Dad give him a big fig of tobacco.

All those who have had dealings with the Australian Aboriginals will smile incredulously at this story. I admit that I never knew of an instance, and my experience of them has been varied, where an Aboriginal has taken up work without asking some kind of recompense, unless under compulsion. Mother attributed it to the delicate state of her health, which was well known to the gins of the tribe, but I am of the opinion that the reason was far deeper seated than that, although I give the black women credit for a womanly instinct towards white mothers.

Rolfe Boldrewood Hollow

It was now my turn to leave home and I got work on the railway. My mate was a sturdy old Yorkshireman named Pearce and the house we lived in was locally known as the Rocky Hut. It was situated at the foot of the Big Hill now known as Hilltop. From Rocky Hut a bridle track leads to the old Police Station situated on the main Southern Road at Bargo. I do not know who built the Rocky Hut, it had no legal claimants and was noted throughout the district as being haunted. Perhaps this was the reason no one claimed it.

With the exception of Pearce, no one could be induced to remain in it overnight, but what I want to impress on my readers is the fact that the description of it and its geographical position tallies in a very remarkable manner with that given by Rolfe Boldrewood of Marsdon's home in his book *Robbery Under Arms*, and also that at the time of which I write, I had neither read nor heard of that famous novel, and I'm quite certain that Pearce hadn't until the day of his death. Pearce's family lived at Colo where he had a selection. This was about sixty miles distant. This fact is only related to that which immediately follows.

Long before Pearce worked at the Big Hill he was working at Bethungra, and the man who worked with him there knew the Big Hill and the Colo country thoroughly. He told Pearce that about seven to ten miles from the Rocky Hut there was a piece of excellent land about 100 acres in extent. He gave him some directions which might help him to find it, at the same time he warned him, unless he hit on the right way in to it he might never find it, because it was situated in a hollow or amphitheatre formed by barren sandstone terraces, and that he would not know it until he saw the change in the timber and grass that would appear like a fringe on its margin. He also told him that if he found a large grey gum tree with the letter 'M' cut deeply into the barrel of it, underneath where it forked about twelve feet from the ground, that he would be on the right track.

Pearce spent many holidays looking for this hollow. He told

me about it and seeing it agreed with the geological conditions that I find inseparable from the patches of woodland that we find in this carboniferous region, I determined to go with him and search for it. We camped out for several days but failed to strike any volcanic country, good, bad or indifferent. It was all sandstone, and to make our disappointment more acute, we found the marked tree. From time to time I continued the search. I believe that the hollow exists. Some people say that Boldrewood's Hollow is Burragorang but if there is anything in the descriptive work or topography of the author of *Robbery Under Arms* that cannot be. But, let us leave this debatable matter.

I was returning home to the farm in Burragorang after one of these fruitless excursions when I met with the following strange adventure. I had descended the wrong point of the range that led into the valley. It was getting dark and I had to trust to luck and the instinct of my sure-footed valley bred brumby to bring me through an awkward position. There was no time to turn back. I must have descended the rocky gorge for about two miles when my horse began to sniff and prick his ears. 'Hello,' thought I, 'there's a precipice here; this means a camp-out, and we won't get home till morning'.

Just then I saw a fire that appeared to be burning in the fork of a tree some distance below. This struck me as peculiar. There were no bush fires about, it was the wrong time of the year to expect one. 'It can't be in the fork,' said I to the pony reflectively. 'I suppose it's because I'm looking down into it from the height above that it appears so. We'll have a look at it, anyhow. It might be a gurder hunter or a shale prospector. If so a billy of tea is a dead cert.' Patting his neck, I urged him forwards over the rocks. We were now on grassy land, one of those terraces you meet on the hillside just below the base of the Hawkesbury rocks. I steered in the direction of the fire that still flickered now and then, through the dark forest trees. 'Whoa, Dingo!' I called to my horse who I thought shied badly but was now standing still. A dark form held his bridle. There was also one on each side of me, and before I had time to say Jack Robertson, I was pulled out of my saddle and made a prisoner.

Intrusion upon a Bora

When I recovered my scattered senses, I found I was in the midst of about forty blackfellows, and in the foreground, pointing at me, evidently enraged, stood King Moyengully. 'What for you knock a-me down like a-this?' I demanded boldly as my nerves would allow, but if I was heard no-one heeded. A big pieallor was going on, and anger was stamped on every face.

I was now firmly bound to a sapling and blackfellows stood in front of me and behind me, armed to the teeth. The one behind me troubled me most for oft had I heard the warning, 'Baal white fellow walkit in front of blackfellow'. Two rows were now formed by the blacks in the same manner that prevailed at the King's election. Fear began to creep over me, but what had I done? The King was now walking up and down between the rows talking low and earnestly. Silent messengers appeared from and disappeared into the forests. Anon one would kneel in the rows but none interrupted nor did a stick crack beneath their feet, which were encased in strange shoes evidently made from feathers in some way or other.

It now dawned upon me that I had innocently invaded one of their sacred temples and then I began to take stock of my surroundings. Several trees were carved from the root upwards to a height of ten feet or more. On the tree in which the sacred fire was burning, and which faced the east, a large bird was carved, an emu, I think it was. Strange herring-bone markings were drawn on the ground. Some, like those seen on the grave trees of common blackfellows, others were more intricate and winding. I also noticed several small mounds, but strangest of all was the life-size clay figure of a man in the centre of the tracings. The usual small fires were many, therefore I could plainly see the rude model of the human being lying prostrate on the ground.

This I took to be some sacrificial emblem and all the old legends and rumours of Moyengully's barbarity, chiefly gathered from the gins, crowded in my mind, and of course added to my anxiety. Before me was a strange judge and jury. What would be the verdict? Had I not seen a similar proceeding? How I cursed myself for not taking more heed of the blacks, and at least having learnt their language. I listened with drops of agony on my forehead, for the grunts that amused me at the coronation of the King, that now had my life in his hands. It came, but whether unanimous or not, I cannot tell. A young man now got up from the row and stood in the aisle facing the King who was at the furthest end of it. Today I would give a fiver to be able to write that speech. He was vehement and excited. My interest was tenfold because he frequently made use of the word 'Queahgang'. I tried to follow the speaker by watching his somewhat frantic gestures. Hope siezed on a possible solution. Was he relating all that the white fellow had done for the Princess? He returned to his place again and the King spoke for a few seconds. I thought that they all grunted, and then the young man rose to his feet and ran to me. My great advocate had not finished. He stood before me and facing the whole line of dusky warriors with the King standing a few paces in front. He piealled for fully five minutes and at times I thought he was telling them that if I was to be killed, they would have to kill him first.

The King answered him with a grunt, somewhat akin to our 'Urgh' and turned away, and then the young man hastened to me. I was now unloosed and beckoned to mount. I did this speedily enough. Without a word being uttered, I was led from the sacred grove, an armed blackfellow on either side of me, and either my executioner or deliverer leading my horse. What was the end going to be? Mustering up my departed courage I asked, 'What for you do this? Me been very good feller alonga you'. No answer. They were all like sphinxes. A quarter of a mile was traversed, when another blackfellow was met. I presumed this was a sentry.

A halt was made and a few words spoken, then he who led me threw the reins over my horse's head and exclaimed 'Yan'. Not waiting to gather the reins in my hands I dug the spurs into poor Dingo, and lying low on his withers, for I thought spears, boomerangs and nullas would be humming after me every second, I rode like one mad, right to my own door.

I learned afterwards that it was our kindness to the Princess Queahgang that saved my life. Love enters the hearts even of the savage and makes the whole world akin. The young blackfellow that cut the wood and drew the water for Mother was my advocate, and who married Queahgang according to the rites of his tribe. I also found out that the illness of Queahgang was brought about by the barbarous ordeal that females are made to undergo before they are allowed to marry. The young man's name was Yerrin (Woolly-headed).

After my adventure I always thought that I had some peculiar yet undeterminable privilege among the Aborigines. On my approach they would talk to each other in low tones and laugh softly. Perhaps I had been initiated in the first degree.

Note: It does not seem to have occurred to Ben Carlon that perhaps the Aboriginals had been 'having him on', and had staged a special performance in order to scare him and ensure that he did not try to pry into secret ceremonies on future occasions; that afterwards they revived the joke and had a quiet laugh about it.

The End of a Culture

For something like four hundred centuries the Gundungurra people lived and hunted on their tribal land, living in harmony with nature and striking a perfect balance with their environment. Then came the white man, and in one short century this once happy group was decimated.

As their hunting grounds were taken from them and turned into farmland the animals that provided food and skins for their cloaks became scarcer and scarcer, and the Aborigines were forced more and more to depend on the charity of white settlers. Therein lay their downfall. When these strong, healthy folk forsook their high protein diet and began to live on 'white-man tucker'—flour, sugar, tobacco and rum, they quickly became obese and lethargic. Possessing little resistance to the white man's diseases they quickly succumbed to tuberculosis, influenza, small pox and venereal diseases such as gonorrhoea and syphilis.

The tribal rituals were abandoned and the elders lost their authority and control over the younger folk. The tribe began to camp on the fringe of the villages and townships, or near the homesteads of the larger properties, where they could cadge handouts. At the time of Moyengully's death in 1858, his people used to camp near 'Abbotsford', the residence of William Redfern Antill, 'Mr Willy' to them, and who used to issue rations to the tribe.

Moyengully was buried nearby, on the bank of Crocodile Creek at a spot known locally as Rumker's Island. In 1893 William Cuneo visited the spot and wrote an account describing the occasion for the Picton Post and Advocate, *a copy of which was donated to the Australian Museum in 1899. Following is an excerpt from the Cuneo article:*

Carved Trees at Picton

W.A. Cuneo

About two-and-a-half miles from Picton and about the same distance from Thirlmere—a very pleasant drive or walk—will bring my readers to the subject of this paper. I am first indebted to an old resident of this district for the information, and second to the kindness of Mr S. Mitchell, of the Thirlmere Hotel, who kindly drove me over to see the last resting place of this famous Aboriginal, well-known to many of the old hands as 'King Mullengully'.

From authentic accounts I am able to fix the date on which this Royal personage laid down his sceptre, and departed to the happy hunting grounds, that according to Aboriginal belief are indicated to earthly mortals by the stars in the firmament, or as they put it, 'The fires of the black men who have been spirited away'—the 12th of October, 1858 (35 years ago).

The exact spot where His Royal Highness reposes was shown to us by Mr Samuel Batcup, a tenant of Mr James, of Upper Picton. The locality is known as Rumker's Island. The grave, as is usual with Aboriginal customs, lies on a point or promontary leading to the shore, or bank of Crocodile Creek, and within view of Barkers Bridge. And almost virgin forests surrounds it. It is unusually large and is very similar in appearance to one I saw sketched by Mr R. Etheridge, of the Australian Museum, at the back of The Hermitage, the well-known estate of Mr J. Hayes on Werriberri Creek.

Two carved trees form his Majesty's tomb stones. Mr Batcup informed me that there were formerly three, which is also a usual custom. The grave lies true north and south, and the carved trees stand at angles from the grave. One, a stringybark tree in good state of preservation, stands due west from the grave at a distance of about twenty feet, and the other (also a stringybark) stands about the same distance south of the grave. The carving is partly overgrown, but otherwise is in good preservation. The position of the other tree (an ironbark) was shown to me by Mr Batcup, who saw it when standing, and is north-west about ten feet from the grave. Nothing of this tree remains. It fell from the roots, and has been cut up for firewood or burnt by bush fires. I was somewhat disappointed at this.

The carvings on this tree, judging from other observations in this direction, would be the most important, being nearest the grave. The carvings on the remaining trees are very different, and equally so to any other I have seen. On the tree west of the grave diamonds are cut and angle lines drawn by incisions made by a tomahawk with considerable skill and almost geometrical precision, the bark being removed in all cases before operations were commenced. They commence about two feet from the ground and extend about four feet up the trunk; they are about fifteen inches wide.

The carvings on the south of the grave are not so artistic, but to my mind are far more important, being more suggestive of hieroglyphical records—which I am inclined to believe they are.

A plate from *Dendroglyphs of New South Wales*. Figs 4 and 5 are by Cuneo

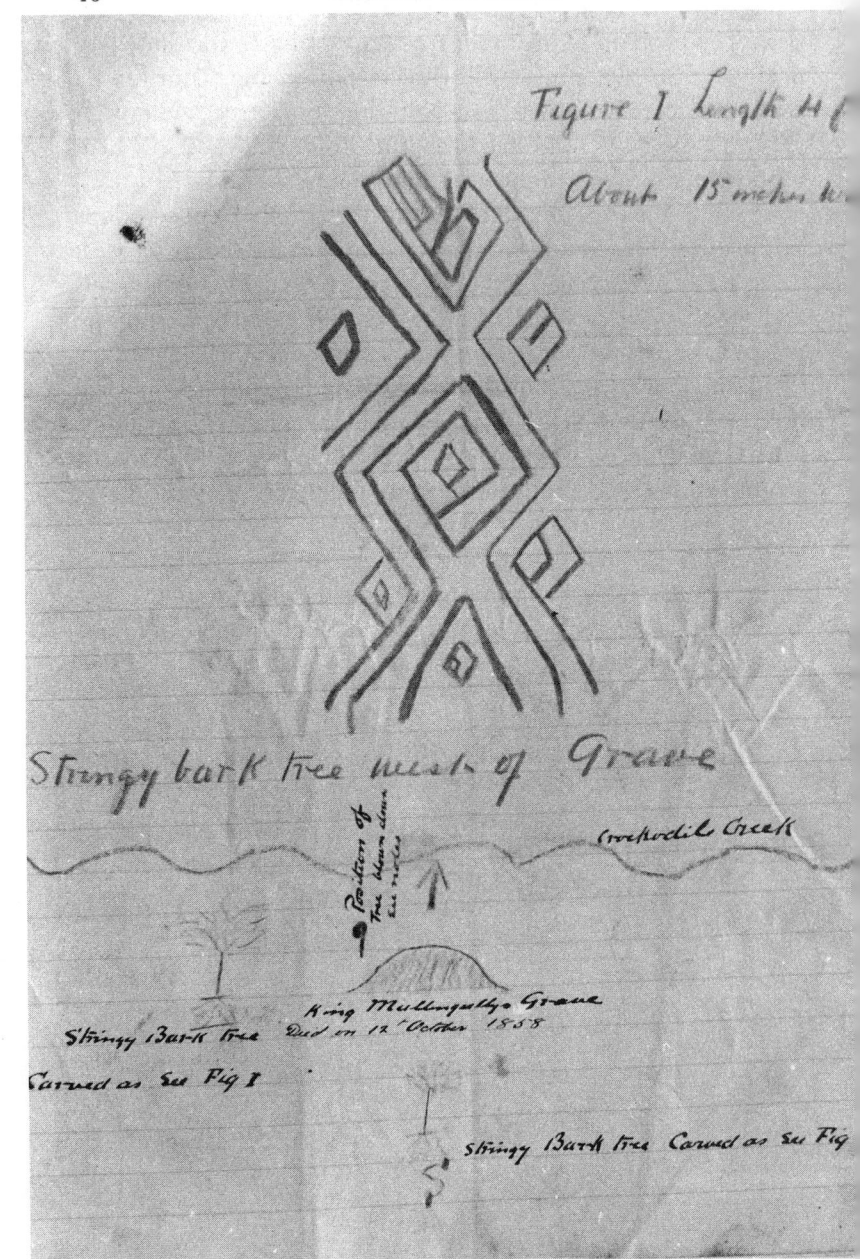

Carving on Moyengully's grave tree, drawn by William Cuneo

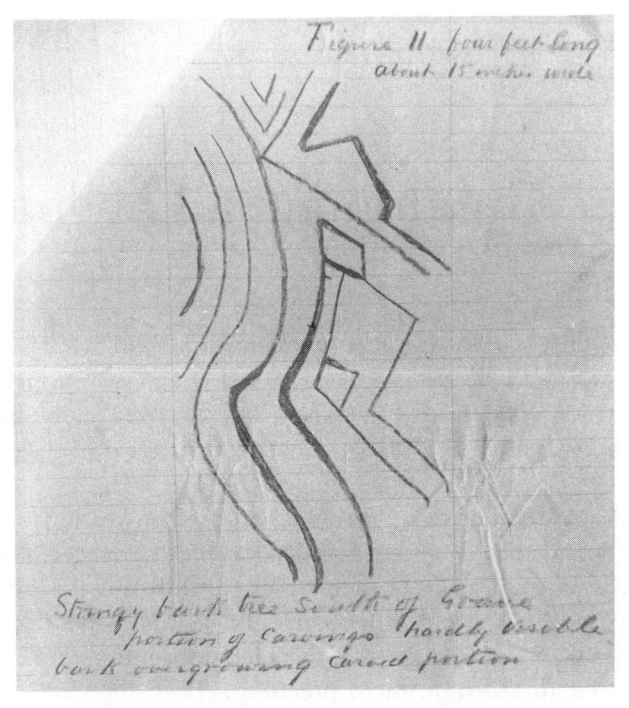

Carving from the second tree

The site of Moyengully's grave, near Picton

The Gundungurra Language

An unwritten language kept alive by oral tradition, must, like a folk song, have developed many variant words. David Collins was aware of this phenomenon and discusses it in his book The English Colony in New South Wales:

'...A sensible difference was often remarked on hearing the same word sounded by two people; and in fact they have been observed sometimes to differ from themselves, substituting the letter 'b' for 'p' and 'g' for 'c', and *vice versa*. In their alphabet they have neither 's' or 'v' and some of their letters would require a new character to ascertain them precisely...'

This could account for the variation in Moyengully's name, Werriberri pronouncing it My-an-garlie, while Cuneo and Carlon say it ought to be Murrungurry. Likewise kooradgie is sometimes given as car-rah-dy.

Bernard O'Reilly, in his autobiographical book Cullenbenbong *writes that:*

'The language of the blacks was not made for white man's tongue and that is why it sounds like blasphemy to hear him try to pronounce an Aboriginal word. The language of wild Australia belongs to wild Australia. Similarly black man's words should never have been put on paper for there is nothing in our alphabet as we understand its sounds which would make the written word any nearer to the original than a feeble parody. A strange thing this language of nature; a haunting echoing softness might give way to unbelievable drama and there were dread words which made your spine creep with horror even though you didn't know their meaning.

'If you listened to the Aborigines speaking together you didn't hear a mumble of foreign words, you heard the sighing of trees, the voice of birds, the sounds of storm and flood and wind, the rolling of rocks in a landslide; you heard stark fear and infinite sadness. There was never joy; that may have always been so, or perhaps because black man's star was setting.

'It is with regret then and some shame that the name Cullenbenbong must be written here; how cold and lifeless it looks in white man's type, yet to hear it pronounced by the black warriors of the old Kanimbla tribe, was to hear majestic thunder re-echoing amongst the granite mountains of their hunting grounds...'

Samuel Bennett notes the similarity of many Aboriginal words to those occurring in the languages of people of Aryan origins that have words descended from the Sanskrit, and quotes a number of examples. One of these, kooradgie *of the Gundungurra which Bennett spells* kiradjee, *is almost identical in a number of other languages:*

Kiradjee	Aboriginal: a doctor
Kheirourgoi	Greek: a doctor
Khoajih	Persian: a doctor
Kiruj (Kirroo)	Danish: a surgeon
Chirurgeon	English: a surgeon
Khiroorg	Russian: a surgeon
Chirurgo	Italian: a surgeon

In An Elementary Grammar of the Gundungurra Tribe, *R.H. Mathews describes the usage of their language in detail. He states that Gundungurra has 19 English letters, comprising 14 consonants:*

$$b\ d\ g\ h\ j\ k\ l\ m\ n\ p\ r\ t\ w\ y$$

and 5 vowels: a e i o u. 'G' is hard, 'r' is rough as in 'hurrah'.

In the following vocabulary, it will be noted that there occur some duplications with variant spelling. This is because the words have been taken from three sources: Major Mitchell, Werriberri (Billy Russell) and A.L. Bennett. The variations are in part from different white men's ideas of writing a sound phonetically, and partly, no doubt, from pronunciation variations in the sub-groups of Aborigines.

Alia	Eat it	Burral	Day
Balbo	Big kangaroo rat	Burrangurang	Grass
Barta	Pipe clay	Burrm-	
Barundi	Yesterday	burrung	Lap-stone
Bendeya	To be full	Burri	Rock wallaby
Benduk	A plain	Burri	Night
Bendy	Abdomen	Burrie	Night
Berack	Dead	Burru	Kangaroo
Berraga	Dead	Burru-ga	Kangaroo bone
Berriga	To laugh		placed through
Bewan	Fat		cartilage of
Bidang	Small scrub wallaby		men's noses
Binaro	Kangaroo	Canbe	Fire
Binure	Old mountain dingo	Cannema	Kangaroo rat
Birriban	Emu	Cappangung	Eggs
Boobal	Boy	Carbundi	A hill at Picton, site
Boolang	Throwing stick		of the Antill
Boombi	Swamp wallaby		family vault
Boombi	A spring or swamp	Carreng	Skin cloak
Boombill-na	Brush turkey	Carreta	Cold
Booro	Kangaroo joey	Carrokang-	
Bootyan	Birds	kang	Ringtail possum
Borre	Four	Cayen	Old man
Branghur	Laughing jackass	Cayingul	Cold
Bubyong	Head	Colaro	Leg
Bucanal	Jag of spear	Colluerr	Three
Budda-wak	Owl	Compelwa	Bustard
Buddayak	Owl	Cookunday	Noise
Budgang	A bird, any bird	Coolayetang	Good
Bulan	A spirit	Coota	Child
Bulber	Red ochre	Coy	Come here
Bulling-gang	Salt water, salt	Cuangy	Stars
Bundil	The sun	Cubbitch	Plenty of
Bundo-luk	The rosella	Cubbitch-	Cowpastures tribe
Bunung	Ashes	barta	(pipe clay,
Bunyal	Sun		plenty)
Buralga	Native companion	Cuckooeang	Cuckoo
Burral	Do not	Cudtakango	Head

Cuikekan	Little squirrel	Golanga ne	Yours
Cumba	Spear	Goolung	Wombat
Cunark	Mud eel, or black eel	Goonama	Snow
		Goo-nar-a-dan	Quail
Cundra-curwa	Cat	Goong-ung	River in flood
Cura-yn	Father	Goorangboon	Butcher-bird
Currar	Long	Gubbu-gang	Eggs
Curratok	Native companion	Guin-daring	Black duck
Curro	Testicles	Gul-guer	Bents Basin (swirl around)
Currobung	A stone		
Curroban	Monkey	Gulung-gooluk	Bullock
Curwur murre	Old woman	Gulla	Of ours
Daoure	Earth	Gum-bal-bal	Native grindstone
Darline	Tongue	Gumbee	Fire
Darra	Thighs	Gumbuck-gooluk	Cow, heifer
Darreng	Hair of the head		
Dictagang	Kingfisher	Gunar	Mountain-top
Dinwere	Perch (fish)	Gun-da-wa	Wallaroo
Dowin	Steel axe	Gunge	Hut
Dulang	A river	Gur-gur	The language of the Cowpastures tribe
Dumbi dumbi	Swamp		
Durra-ma	Right hand		
Durra-mu-lan	An evil spirit	Gurrimocko	Deaf
		Gurungadge	Dreamtime giant eel spirit
Dyenna	Foot		
Engaetyung	Sea	Gurungatch	Dreamtime giant eel spirit
Gabugan	Eggs		
Gadung	The sea	Irri-bi-gang	Swallow (bird)
Gammuang	Mother	Irribingang	Swallow (bird)
Garragin	No	Jakular	Lyrebird
Garraguin	Bad	Jerra	Stars
Gerarc	Gill bird	Kanga	Neck
Gerre-gang	Black magpie	Karrat	Rain
Gil-ber-ark	Skylark	Kinyeac	Black swan
Gilwidge	Black snake	Kurang	Cloud
Gimbil	Spark	Kurra-gang	Magpie
Gin-yuk	Swan	Kurre	Ears
Gkinno	Feet	Maandoo	Bandicoot
Gnamaiko	The heart	Magurrung	Crayfish
Gnaetyung	To be thirsty	Maikatong	Swan
Gne	Yes	Makileiko	Eyes
Gnollieng	Possum-wool girdle	Malyal	Eagle
Gola n ga ya	Mine	Mando	Bandicoot

Marrola	Hand	Narre-gar-	
Marrup	Lightning	rang	Picton Lakes
Mayap	Lightning	Narroan	Young man
Me	Sinews	Nogorra	Nose
Medung	One	Norrongho	Arms
Mee-oo-wun	Mount Mouin	Nubba	Knife or sharp
Melanghan	Eel		edged stone
Menimgha eu-ya pattowa koko pelin	Little-fellow-fly-away	Nulla-bunya-gang	Wood duck
		Numbuk	Smoke
		Nyamburro nega	To sleep
Merrigang	Dog		
Mewer-re	Emu	Ny-apung	Mamillæ
Mibbi	Mullet	Nyuna	Elbow
Midger	Sharp edge of stone axe	Nye	Ghost, spirit
		Nyerriayn	Plenty
Mil	Eyes	Ooalle	Possum
Mirra	Left hand	Pala-an	Platypus
Mirragang	Common dingo	Par	Whiskers
Mirri-gang ambero	Dingoes, a lot	Parowra	Shoulders
		Pelin-kang	Flying squirrel
Moyolong	Large eel	Piang	Large
Mudgerwik	Death adder	Porrende	Tomorrow
Mugga	Any snake	Pudtanbang	Duck
Mulla-da	Big stone axe	Pulla	Two
Mullyang	Eagle	Tamulo	Muscles
Mundo	Bandicoot	Taourey	Buried
Mundo	Mouth	Theulda	To be hungry
Muringo	Ribs	Tintak	Swan
Murrin	A man	Tonbero	Tail
Murrin-bil	Peewit	Tooluan	A river
Murringh	Ribs	Thura, or Thurra	Old woman
Murro-lung-gulung	Red hand stencils in a cave		
		Tyeluck	Moon
Murrongul	Thunder	Tyerra weet	Black snake
Murrowa-longho		Waak	Fish
	Hard	Wagga	Small blackfish
Murruging	Native cat	Wagul	Diamond snake
Murungnal	Thunder	Wam-bee-ang	Wombeyan Caves
Mutoit	Knee	Wambuyn	Kangaroo
Nadgyung	Water	Wan-dak-ma-lai	Duckmulloy
Nain	Men		
Nao	Liver	Warbin	Curlew

Warrabing	Curlew	Worrgun	Whip snake
Warre mugo	Short	Worrigal	Dog
Warrong	Pademelon	Wurrumbul	Wood duck
Wella	Possum	Yabbun	A corroboree
Wenyo	Hot	Yadte	Scarce
Wenyo nyam-burraniga	To make a hut	Yarreng	The beard
		Yengo	Now
Werrika	Goanna	Yerra	Teeth
Werrimbi	Flying fox	Yerra ba (waving hand)	Go away!
Wilhe	Possum		
Winu	Hot		
Wogolin	Crow		
Wongwa malingang pokarre moikke wakarra	Black cockatoo	Yerra bunya	I go away
		Yerra-mang	Horse
		Yoko	Sweetbreads

Gundungurra Mythology: Mirragan and Gurangatch

Taken down by R.H. Mathews from remnants of the tribe residing on the Wollondilly River in Burragorang Valley and published by him in 1908.

In the far past times, in the gun-yung-ga-lung, all the present animals were men, or at any rate had human attributes. These legendary personages are spoken of as the Burringilling, in contradistinction to the present race of people. It would appear however, that the Burringilling folk were much cleverer than the people of the present time. They could make rivers and other geographical features, cleave rocks and perform many similar Herculean labours.

Gu-rang-atch was one of the Burringilling, his form being partly fish and partly reptile. One of his camping places was in a large, deep waterhole or lagoon at what is now the junction of the Wollondilly and Wingeecaribee rivers; the waterhole and the country around it being called Mur-rau-ral in the Gundungurra tongue. Gurungatch used to lie in the shallow water near the bank in the middle of the day to sun himself. One day Mir-ra-gan the tiger cat, a renowned fisherman, who searched only for the largest kinds of fish, happened to catch a glimpse of Gurangatch's eye which shone like a star through the water. Mirragan tried to spear him but he escaped into the centre of the waterhole, which was of great depth. Mirragan then went into the bush a little way off, and cut a lot of hickory bark, called Millewa in the native language, and stacked it in heaps under the water at different places around the lagoon, in the hope of making Gurangatch sick, so that he would come to the surface. (There are some long, thin slabs of stone still lying in layers on the banks of Murraural waterhole, which are the sheets of hickory bark put there by Mirragan to poison the water.) The poisoned water made Gurangatch very uncomfortable, but the solution was not strong enough to overcome such a large fish as he.

Seething with disappointment, Mirragan went into the bush again to cut more hickory bark to increase the nauseating power of the water, but as soon as Gurangatch saw him going away he suspected what he was after and commenced tearing up the ground along the present valley of the Wollondilly, causing the water in the lagoon to flow after him and bear him along. He went on forming several miles of the river channel, and then he burrowed or tunnelled under the ground for some distance at right angles, coming out again on a high, rocky ridge on one side of the valley, where there is now a spring or water catchment, known to the white people as 'Rocky Waterhole', but is called by the natives Bir-rim-bun-nung-a-lai, because it contains birrimbunnungs or sprats. The natives say that there is a subterraneous passage from Rocky Waterhole to the Wollondilly because sprats are found there as well as in the river. Gurangatch raised his head above this waterhole and shoved out his tongue which flashed like lightning. From this elevated point of observation he saw Mirragan starting from Murraural along his trail.

Gurangatch then returned along his burrow or tunnel to the Wollondilly where he had previously left off, and continued making a canal for himself. When he reached what is now the junction of Guineacor River he turned to the left and made a few miles of the channel of that stream. Coming to a very rocky place which was hard to excavate, he changed his mind and turned back to the junction and resumed his former course. He had some difficulty in getting away from this spot and made a long, deep bend or loop in the Wollondilly which almost doubles back upon itself at that place. When Gurangatch got down to where Jock's Creek now embouchures with the Wollondilly, he turned up Jock's Creek excavating a watercourse for himself.

Being a great magician he could make water flow uphill as easily as downhill. On reaching the source of Jock's Creek, he burrowed under the range, coming up in the inside of Wam-bee-ang caves, which are now called Whambeyan by the white people, being a corruption of the Aboriginal name.

We must now return to Mirragan. When he came back to Murraural waterhole and saw how Gurangatch had escaped, he followed on down the river after him, going on and on till he overtook him at Wambeeang. Mirragan did not care to go into any of the subterranean passages, therefore he went up on top of the rocks and dug a hole as deep as he could go and then prodded a long pole down as far as it would reach, for the purpose of frightening Gurangatch out of his retreat, much in the way we poke a kangaroo-rat or other creatures out of a hollow log. Not succeeding in his purpose with the first hole, he dug another and still another and shoved the long pole down each one as before. There are still several weather-worn 'pot holes' on top of the Whambeyan caves, which are said to be those made by Mirragan on that occasion.

When Gurangatch perceived that his enemy was continuing his relentless pursuit, he started off one morning at daylight through his tunnel or burrow and returned down Jock's Creek till he came out into the Wollondilly again. Some miles farther down was where Mirragan's family resided. When they heard Gurangatch coming and the water roaring after him like a flood, they ran away up the side of the hill in great terror. By that time Mirragan himself appeared upon the scene and his wife began scolding him for having meddled with Gurangatch and besought him to give up the pursuit, but he would not be dissuaded. He went on after Gurangatch and overtook him at what the white people call the 'Slippery Rock', but the native name is Woong-ga-ree. There they fought for a long time, which made the rock smooth and slippery ever since.

Gurangatch at last got away and went on downwards, making the water flow after him. Every time that Mirragan overtook him, he hit him with his big club or boondee, and Gurungatch struck Mirragan heavily with his tail. This continued down to what is now the junction of Cox's River, where Gurangatch turned off to the left, digging out the present channel. He went on till he came to Billa-goo-la Creek, corrupted to 'Black Hollow' on our maps, up which he travelled some distance, but turned back and resumed his course up the Cox to the junction of Kedoom-bar Creek, now called Katoomba by the Europeans. He excavated Kedoombar Creek as far up as where Reedy Creek comes into it and turned up the latter a little way, where he formed a deep waterhole in which he rested for a while.

Gurangatch then journeyed back to the Cox, up which he worked his way for some distance and formed the waterhole Karrangatta. In order to dodge his enemy he burrowed underground, coming out on Mee-oo-wun mountain, now written Mou-in, where he made a deep hole or spring, which is even now a menace to the white man's cattle on account of its narrowness and great depth. Returning to Karrangatta waterhole, he made his way up to the junction of Koo-nang-goor-wa, corrupted to Konangaroo, where he and Mirragan had another fierce encounter. Gurangatch journeyed on up the Cox to the present junction therewith of Harry's Creek. He then excavated the valley of Harry's Creek till he came to Bin-noo-mur, the present Jenolan caves, where he had the good fortune to meet with some of his relations.

Gurangatch was weary from his hard work and sore from all the blows he had received during his journey. He suspected that his enemy would still be in pursuit of him and therefore besought his friends to escort him out of his reach. They accordingly took him out of the caves and conducted him over the main range into a deep waterhole, called by the natives Joo-lun-doo.

While this was going on, Mirragan had arrived close to Binnoomur, but was very tired and lay down on a little hill to rest himself. When he revived he searched about the caves and found tracks of where Gurangatch had been staying, and also the tracks of how he had been taken away to Joolundoo by his friends. Mirragan was quite worn out by his prolonged encounter, and when he saw that his quarry had got among his relations, he thought that he also would go and obtain assistance.

He then considered that it would be prudent, before he left the spot, to adopt some means of preventing Gurangatch from escaping back to his old haunts during his absence. He consequently set to work and built a precipitous wall of rock, Wan-dak-ma-lai, corrupted by Europeans to Duckmulloy, along the side of the range between the caves and Joolundoo. A precipitous sandstone escarpment, consisting of huge blocks of rock, layer upon layer, is still pointed out as the wall built by Mirragan.

Mirragan then hurried away to his friends somewhere out westward. On reaching their camp they were eating roasted eels and offered him one. Although he was weary and hungry he answered, 'No, no, that is too small a thing for me to eat. I am chasing a great big fish and want you to come and help me.' He stated that this great fish was in an extremely deep waterhole and requested them to send the very best divers in the camp. They selected Billagoola the shag, Gool-a-gwan-gwan the diver, Gundhareen the black duck and Goonarring the wood duck.

When Mirragan returned to Joolundoo with this contingent, Gundhareen dived into the pool but returned after a while saying he was unable to get down to the bottom. Goonarring then made the attempt but without success. Goolagwangwan was the next to go down and after a considerable time brought a young or small Gurangatch to the surface, saying to Mirragan, 'Is this what you have been after?' 'No! That is too small; try again.' Goolagwangwan dived down the second time and brought up a larger fish, but Mirragan would not look at it. Billagoola then took his turn at diving and when he got down a long way, he observed several fish like those brought up by Goolagwangwan. They were trying to hide a very large fish by covering it with mud on the bottom of the pool. Billagoola tried to get hold of this monster, but its head was jammed into a crevice of the rock and its tail was fast in another crevice on the opposite side, so that he could not shift it. Being a very expert diver and a strong fellow withal, he pulled a huge piece of flesh off the back of Gurangatch and started up again. On reaching the surface, Mirragan exclaimed with delight, 'That is a piece of the fish

I was chasing.' When the meat was cooked Mirragan and his friends had a great feast and returned to their respective homes.

Along the course of the Wollondilly, as well as along the Cox river, there are big waterholes here and there, which are said by the natives to be Gurangatch's resting places. The following are some of the holes in the Wollondilly: Doogalool, Gungga-look, Woonggaree, Goo-rit, Mullindee, Boonbaal and Gurrabulla. In the Cox river there are Gaung-gaung, Junba, Billagoola, Karrangatta, and several others. Many of the waterholes referred to are believed by the old natives to be inhabited to the present day by descendants of Gurangatch.

Anthology

As well as writing articles about the Gundungurra people, and about 'Mullengully's' grave, William Cuneo, on occasion, was inspired to write verse about Yerranderie, the Burragorang Valley, and the burial spot of Moyengully. On his visit to the site in 1893 he made sketch copies of the two remaining tree carvings, copies of which were sent to Robert Etheridge who included them on Plate 31 of his book Dendroglyphs or Carved Trees of New South Wales. *The original drawings were then donated by him to the Australian Museum in Sydney, where they are preserved. After making his sketches, Cuneo was moved to compose an ode:*

An Ode on King Murrungurry's Grave

Sleep on dusky King in thy grass-hidden grave,
   'Neath the shade of the forest lie many a brave
That has bowed to thy sceptre, no homage denied,
   When thy kingdom unconquered on valor relied.

Ah! if thy dark spirit that 'Twans' carried high,*
   To rest by the fires on the dome of the sky
Could return for a moment, thy kingship resume,
   And relate for thy country what's writ on thy tomb.

Ah! would that I knew, at our doubts you may smile,
   But those queer hieroglyphics—such are seen on the Nile;
Tell of valor, of grandeur, a past we'll ne'er see,
   Is thy life here recorded on yon drooping tree?

---

* 'Twans': Spirits who take the form of birds. They are supposed to carry off the spirit of the dead.

Perhaps 'tis the story, tho' I dream and surmise,
  Of the deeds thou hast done ere thy fame could arise;
How of tribes thou hast conquered, the lives thou hast sealed
  With thy boomerang, spear and thy womerah shield.

Sleep on thou Royal Savage, thy tribe is no more,
  P'raps locked in thy bosom lay historical lore;
A bard asks a favour, Yes! I crave it of thee,
  Let thy tombstone be sacred—yon stringybark tree.

W.A. Cuneo

Recollections *by Billy Russell consists of the reminiscences of Werriberri, written down for him and published by Mr A.L. Bennett, 'Spring Hills', Glenmore, on 16 February 1914. In his foreword Bennett says of Werriberri: '...I have ever had a veneration for the fast-disappearing Australian Aborigine, of which Russell is about the last of his tribe, and is certainly by far the oldest native of this district.' A.L. Bennett's brother, S.V. Bennett, in 1903 wrote a poem titled 'The Blackfellow's Grave', which might perhaps have been inspired by Moyengully's burial place. Their father, Samuel Bennett, wrote a five volume* History of Australian Discovery and Colonisation, *published in 1865.*

The Blackfellow's Grave

No marble marks this resting place,
No artist here has stopped to trace
The sculptured words of woe;
No gilded organ pipes are here,
Naught but the wild bird's note we hear
Or the wind murmuring low.

There are no sable hatchments shown,
No weeping seraphims in stone
Above this sylvan grove;
No towers or spires overhead,
But lofty gums their branches spread
And mournful grasstrees wave.

The wild flowers bloom about the place,
Sad token of a vanished race,
Vanished, Ah! Who may know!
O! Pass not by with careless tread
The sacred ashes of the dead,
The dead of long ago.

                                              S.V. Bennett, 1903

'Princess Betsy'

Where now the gum-tree sheds its leaves,
    And the golden wattles bloom;
And the Goddess Flora softly weaves
    A native wreath o'er Betsy's tomb.

       Epitaph by Harry Peckman, the Blue Mountains Poet

The Blue Mountains Echo *of 21 February 1919 carried an account of how James Neale, the first settler in the area, tried to learn the Aboriginal name of the place. With this end in view he sought out, and entertained at a picnic, 'Princess Betsy' of the Kanimbla tribe, then camped at Hartley. She told him it was 'Katumba' which referred to a local waterfall, and so Katoomba got its name. It is possible that this lady was the same person referred to by Ben Carlon as 'Princess Queahgang'. The picnic took place in the 1870s.*

A Bushman's Experience

It was a cold, frosty morning when we shouldered our pick
And left Camden for Burragorang, myself, Jack and Mick;
We passed down a steep, rocky mountain, a mighty cold
    place,
Where the bush and scrub tore the bark off our face.
Arriving, Moingang, chief of Burragorang and king of
    Aborigines was there,

He was wearing a nice crown cap made of skin of a bear.
We told him we were tired, hungry, footsore and cold,
And came to Burragorang to prospect for gold.

Moingang wished us good luck and expressed a desire
To give us a warm welcome, he asked his people to light up
  a big fella buggerie fire;
By that fire we had a good talk,
And he gave us a good meal of damper and wild piggie
  pork.
Just about midnight made a dos on the ground,
And I can assure you we slept very sound.

All our dreams were about gold,
We knew it bright yellow, hard and cold.
Next day we built our humpy, one we found very cold,
We went about the river, digging for gold.
The work was hard and the prospects were poor,
So we started a little farm and garden for our living to be
  sure.
The birds and marsupials and other pests, you know,
They never let much in our garden grow.

There was a snow white thieving cockatoo, he's cunning, he's
  shy,
You cannot capture him, no matter how you try.
His visits are very early with the watchman perched up
  high,
And gives others a warning and away they all do fly.
Then there's the wilie possum, he plants in a tree spout,
Visits the garden on a dark night when there's nobody
  about.
Round our little humpy we had a pair of broken delft
Which left it on the possum for he tracked her on the shelf.

There's a rusty-musty ginger fox, he sneaks about very shy,
He captured all our little pullets and made the little
  Shanghai rooster cry;

There's a howling prowling dingo, he's a pest upon the run
And kills a pair of jumbugs mostly for the fun;
He feasts upon the mutton that's young and not too old,
There's the stringybark goanna, he ambles up so gay,
And chases the old hen and rooster, he swallows all the eggs and then swaddles away.

There's the cruel, cruel black crow, his cruel doings would make you cry
For every poor old beast down, he picks out their eye.
Then there's the little parrot, he's about early in the morn,
He doesn't destroy the garden, but he loves the cob of corn;
There's the harmless humpy-stumpy ugly bear, neither white or black,
He climbs the highest gum tree with a young one on his back.
There's the canny, bonny rabbit, he's very distinctive, you know,
And forces on a terrible drought and lays the country to waste.

By law we're forced to destroy him, and we all here done our best,
You know he broke all squatters away out west.
Great big game we hunted about the mountain top,
And we can tell you about the kangaroos, and how they used to hop;
We had a number almost captured, when the leader took a slew,
And we got tangled up with old man Aussie kangaroo;
With sticks and stones we fought him right up to the rising of the moon,
Between Jack, Mick and myself, and the old man King's coon.

How the battle ended now I'll tell you true,
We had a good supply of mutton off the old man kangaroo.
Great snakes! We used for fencing poles and porcupine for chock,

In order to enclose a feeding place for poor old horsey Jock;
But the wallaroo and wallaby hop high and really laugh,
Scaling over our snake-proof fence to eat the horse's chaff.

Now I've given you the dinkum figures of boys the story that I've told,
If you go prospecting in Burragorang, you'll get mighty little gold,
And don't venture down the Devil's Gate, where the Kowmung River below,
For there's wild animals of all descriptions, very treacherous and fierce, you know;
There's a great, tall, black, hairy man we call the Bennicia Bull,
Hear his thundering voice rolling thru the mountain, and the echo comes back and says
'I'm the King of Burragorang and you'd better keep away!'

The trees grow very tall in the Kowmung, they grow right towards the sky,
In which the mighty eagle builds his nest and the young ones they do cry.
Higher in the Darby, higher in the day,
Higher in the Darby, 'twas on the Darby Day.

Joe Feld, Upper Burragorang

Notes: This unusual piece of doggerel verse was sent to me by that indefatigable researcher of Burragorang Valley history, Ron Mills. Leo Rideout and Val Luedi had drawn his attention to it in the Camden News *of 19 May 1949. Folk song references and one quote, such as 'The Rising of the Moon', 'The Bold Bennicia Boy' and 'The Darby Ram', suggest that Joe Feld may also have been a singer.*

Like the Cuneo stories, which turned out to be the adventures of Ben Carlon, this ballad could perhaps concern the activities of somebody other than Joe, as is suggested by the text. Feld was born in 1860, and could reasonably be expected to be between 15 and 20 years of age at the very least when he went prospecting, which would put it about 1875 to 1880.

Reference is made to Mongang, King of the Burragorang and his 'coon'. In the 1838 Returns of Native Aborigines, Mongang (or Moingang) is recorded as having two wives and two children, a boy and a girl. By the time Joe Feld was old enough to go prospecting with his brothers, Mongang's son would have been in his late 30s, and rather old to be referred to as a 'coon'. Mongang is listed in the Return for 1838, but his name is missing from the subsequent Return of 1842 which was carried out at Picton. He may have died in the interim, and so Joe Feld's verse-narrative could have been based on the experiences of one of the original pioneers of the Burragorang Valley.

Bibliography

Australian Museum, Minute Paper, 'W.A. Cuneo, Subject: Carved Trees.' C84/1899.
Bennett, Samuel, *History of Australian Discovery and Colonisation.*
Bennett, S.V., poem, 'The Blackfellow's Grave'.
Brereton, John le Gay, papers, 'A. Cuneo, 1860-1942'.
Camden News, 19 May 1949.
Carmody, Jean, *Early Days of the Upper Murray.*
Cuneo, William Albert, 'A Brain Record'—a typescript account in the Mitchell Library.
——'Murrungurry, a Great Kooradgie.' Included in 'A Brain Record'.
——'Lines on Sketching King Mullungurry's Grave.' Included in above.
——'When Murrungurry was King.' Included in above.
Everitts, M.M., *The Organisation, Language and Initiation Ceremonies of the Aborigines.*
Feld, Joe, poem, 'A Bushman's Experience'. In *Camden News*, above.
Fraser, John, 'Aborigines of N.S.W. 1892.'
Govett, W.R., manuscript notebook, 1828-35.
Etheridge, Robert, *Dendroglyphs or Carved Trees of New South Wales*, 1918.
Historical Records of N.S.W., Vol. 3, pp.820-28, John Price/Barrack's Diary of Wilson's Expeditions, 1798.
Jervis, James, *A History of the Berrima District 1798-1973.*
McAllister, Charles, *Old Pioneering Days in the Sunny South.*
Matthews, R.H., *An Elementary Grammar of the Gundungurra Tribe.*
——*Mythology of the Gundungurra Tribe.*
——*The Bunan Ceremony of Initiation.*
Mills, Ron, a letter to Mills from the Archives Officer of the State Rail Authority regarding W.A. Cuneo.
Mitchell, Sir Thomas L., Field Note Book 1828-30.
——*Three Expeditions into the Interior of Eastern Australia*, 1838.
O'Reilly, Bernard, *Cullenbenbong*, 1944.
Peck, C.W., *Aboriginal Legends of the Burragorang Valley.*
Russell, Billy, *My Recollections*, Camden, 1914.
Wyatt, Ransome T., *The History of Goulburn*, 1941.

Appendix

'Return of Aboriginal Natives' was the quaint name given to a four-yearly census of Aborigines carried out by district magistrates. The purpose of the census was twofold—to keep a tally on the population levels, and to bring the Aborigines in to an administrative centre for the issue of free blankets supplied by the government.

The blankets were issued at the rate of one for each adult, and one for every two children. The form of the return set out the name, age, sex and marital status of each person, and recorded both the tribal name and the white-man name. The following aggregate figures represent a summarisation of the returns in the Picton district for 1834, 1838 and 1842.

'Return of Aboriginal Natives' in the Picton area,
1834, 1838 and 1842.

Aggregate figures:

Brownlow Hill, 1 June 1834.	Males	15
	Females	24
	Children	14
	Total	53

'Murringully'. Probable age 46; 3 wives, 1 daughter; Burragorang Tribe of the District of Burragorang and Nattai.

Stonequarry, 27 April 1838.	Males	27
	Females	23
	Children	13
	Total	63

'King Murringully'. Probable age 50; 2 wives, 1 daughter. Nattai Tribe; District of usual resort, Burragorang.

Picton, 6 August 1842.	Males	30
	Females	18
	Children	13
	Total	61

'Morangully'. English name, 'The King'. Probably age, 40; 2 wives, 1 daughter. Designation of the tribe: Burragorang–Nattai and Coxes River Tribe. District of usual resort, The Oaks, principally about Vanderville.

Men	Women	Children	Total	Year
15	24	14	53	1834
27	23	13	63	1838
30	18	13	61	1842

Index

Abbotsford, 15, 43
Antill, W.R., 15, 35, 43

Backhouse, Jas., 10
Barrallier, 12
Batcup, Mr, 44-5
Bennett, A.L., 21, 50, 61
Bennett, Dr George, 10, 12
Bennett, S.V., 61
Bennett, Samuel, 49, 61
Betsy, Princess, see *Queahgang*
Big Hill, 38
Boldrewood, Rolph, 38
Bora, 40
Bradley, Wm., 9

Carlon, Ben, 14, 15, 30
Carmody, Jean, 13
Collins, David, 48
Connors Plains, 16
Cox River, 57, 59
Crocodile Creek, 43-4
Cuneo, W.A., 14, 30, 43, 60

Dowle, Roy, 24
Duckmolloy, 58

Edwards River Tribe, 32
Etheridge, R., 44

Feld, Joe, 65-6

Goulburn, 12
Goulburn Plains, 11, 12
Govett, W.R., 20
Gurangatch, 54

Hayes, J., 44
Hermitage, The, 44
Hilltop, 38
Hume, Hamilton, 8

Jarvisfield, 15
Jenolan Caves, 57

Kangaroo Song, 18

Lynch, Billy & Fanny, 28
Luedi, Val, 65

McAlister, Chas, 9
McArthur, John, 12
Macquarie, Gov., 8
Mathews, R.H., 49, 54
Mills, Ron, 65
Mirragan, 54
Mitchell, Mr S., 44
Michell, Maj. T.L., 10, 13, 15, 16, 20, 50
Mongang/Moingang, 66
Moyengully, 7, 15-17, 19, 20, 23, 31, 34, 40, 43
Muroon/Murruin, 23, 35
Murrundah, 25

O'Reilly, Bernard, 27, 48

Peckman, Harry, 62
Picton, 44

Queahgang, Princess, 31, 36, 41-2, 62

Rideout, Leo, 65
Road Song, 18
Rumkers Island, 43
Russell, Billy, see *Werriberri*

Thirlmere, 44
Twan, 37

Waugh, Dr, 13
Werriberri, 11, 23-4, 27, 50
Whambeyan/Wombeyan Caves, 56
Wilson, John, 16
Wollondilly, 59
Wonduk, 23

Yarraginny, 13
Yerrin, 42